MY EMOTIONS AND ME:
A Guide for Youth and Their Caregivers

Dr. Free

To order additional copies of this book, contact:
Xlibris
844-714-8691
www.Xlibris.com
Orders@Xlibris.com

ISBN: Softcover   978-1-6641-8046-8
         EBook   978-1-6641-8045-1

Print information available on the last page

Rev. date: 06/24/2021

CONTENTS

MY EMOTIONS AND ME

*There are lots of emotions to feel other than just happy or sad
for this, I've decided I'm grateful and truly glad.
Kids know so but don't usually say so
That's the way their stories typically go*

All kinds of emotions are possible in between

Adults sense their importance--giving moods and moments with friends and family deeper meaning

Emotions add color to our lives

Flavor to our tries and hope to our whys

Emotions add a tangy twist to bittersweet good-byes

Our emotions are natural and useful for us not weird or strange or wrong or right

Our emotions are like a dial we turn that dims or brightens our inner light

The emotional part of us is like our own ready compass for guiding our life

Each day is different, terrific and brand new
Old feelings new ones never ever a few

So, the way our emotions make us feel isn't always familiar
But, wait—know this, neither are our feelings ever peculiar

Our feelings are personal proof of a need or an expression
of what we believe
Our feelings are a reflection for what our heart truly sees

I'm still learning to respond emotionally with wisdom
My emotions serve me and bring about clear vision
So I do not dupe myself or ignore my emotional help
with mindfulness I pay attention and help myself!

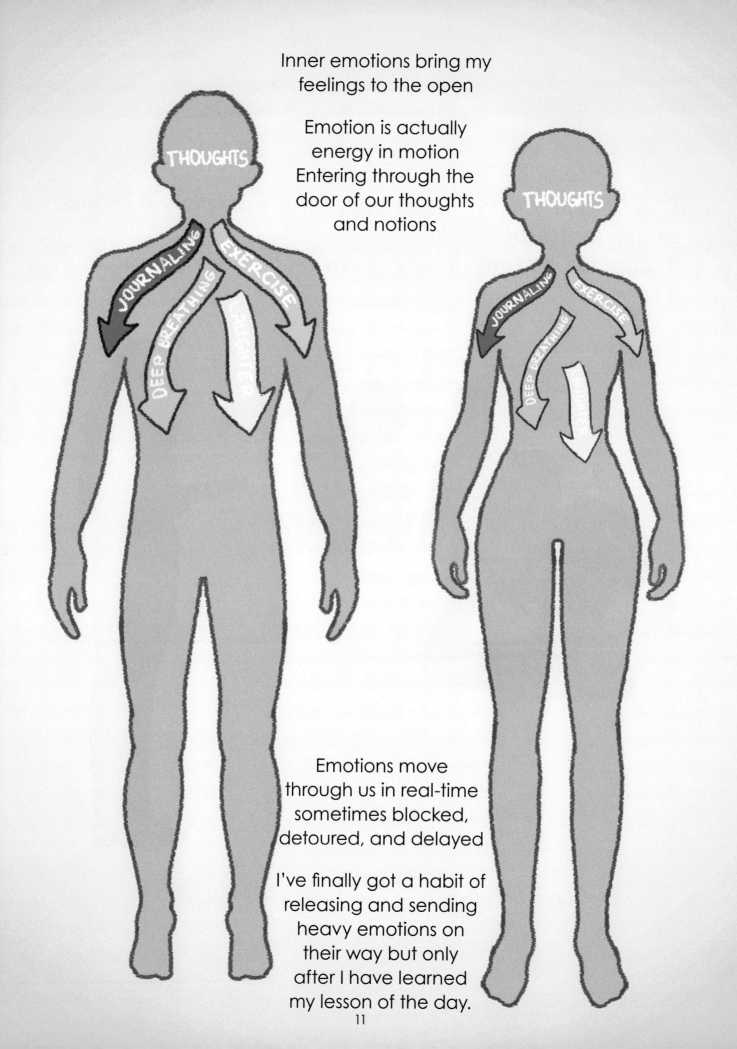

Inner emotions bring my
feelings to the open

Emotion is actually
energy in motion
Entering through the
door of our thoughts
and notions

Emotions move
through us in real-time
sometimes blocked,
detoured, and delayed

I've finally got a habit of
releasing and sending
heavy emotions on
their way but only
after I have learned
my lesson of the day.

11

Don't judge yourself if you happen to experience shame,
anger, guilt, fear, or grief
Recognize it, sit with it-asking why it's here—then transform
it for relief

Feeling good means high vibrations--making me happy, healthy, and strong
When my vibe is low for too long something is bound to go wrong

Emotions are natural and useful for me not weird or strange or wrong or right
Emotions are like a dial I turn that dims or brightens my inner light
The emotional part of me is like my own ready compass for guiding my life

My emotions help me survive,

My emotions make me thrive, feel alive, and enjoy good times

My emotions move me to connect to others I see, think before I leap, and show compassion for those in need

Beware! Untethered anger erupts like a volcano hurling hot lava all over the place
Barging itself into soft, fragile, unwelcomed and sacred spaces
On the other hand, stuffing my emotions down inside
Never diminishes the power of the feelings I'm trying to hide
My feelings will come out somewhere somehow at some time by surprise

Visit Nature

Deep Breathing

Break for fun

Exercise

So, releasing anger in a safe way and in a safe place with intention
Keeps me from apologizing for harmful acts and words I regretfully mentioned

When I sense my emotions as they rise from inside
I'm the only one who decides
how I choose to feel

Oh and when my desire matches what I feel
My wildest dreams can become real

My emotions may alert me a change is necessary
I must remember how I feel is most important
Never secondary

Kids who feel the warmth of acceptance and the comfort of unconditional love tend to authentically do amazing things That's just the wonderful result our feelings can bring

Adults who have an awareness of how they feel can begin
to deeply heal old pains and trauma from the past
For a lifetime hurt does not have to last

*Our emotions are natural and useful
for us not weird or strange or wrong
or right
Our emotions are like a dial we turn
that dims or brightens our inner light
The emotional part of us is like our own
ready compass for guiding our life*

❧ REFLECTION QUESTIONS

For Youth

You will need a journal or notebook and pen/pencil to record your thoughts as you answer the reflection questions.

Read the reflections questions at a pace that is best for you.

Our feelings and emotions help us to understand ourselves better. They can alarm us when things are not quite right and energize us when we're having fun. A person who is aware of how he or she feels can live life **authentically**. Living authentically means behaving in a way that is sincere, honest, and true to self.

1. Many words can describe how we feel other than just happy or sad. Words that describe our emotions have shades of meaning. Read the chart of sample words and their different shades of meaning that more precisely describe feelings.

sad	disappointed	annoyed	upset	angry	furious
attentive	alert	awake	sleepy	tired	exhausted
elated	excited	cheerful	happy	content	well

Now, make a list of five common words that you regularly use to describe your feelings. Use a dictionary to gain more understanding of each word. Also, a thesaurus can help add other words to your emotional vocabulary. For example, the word unwanted means no longer desired. Similar words can be found for the word **unwanted** in a thesaurus: **dislike, undesirable, unacceptable, offensive. dreadful, disgusting.** The activity will help you identify and express your emotions more clearly.

2. The next time you experience an emotion take a moment to name it. This is especially useful with strong emotions. Identify strong emotions like jealousy, anger, or anxiety as you experience them by naming them. **"I am feeling _____."** This is the first step toward directing your thoughts and actions in a way that helps you recognize what you are feeling and solve problems. **"I am feeling _____, because _____.**
There are times when you may need help with managing strong emotions. You can ask your parent, teacher, friend, or an adult you trust for help. Read and familiarize yourself with the examples below. *Use these statements to express what you need to people you trust.*

I need to talk.
I need you to listen to me.
I need to be alone.
I need to leave.
I need a hug.
I need some help.
I need more time.
I need you to sit with me.

3. Emotions keep life from being boring. The emotions we experience teach us about who we are. We may have similar feelings as others sometimes, but our **emotional expressions** are personal. Being emotionally unique is wonderful! We never have to be ashamed or embarrassed when we feel different from others. Have you ever been the only one crying, irritated, laughing, or angry? Our **emotional individuality** typically shows up most when we are learning something new about ourselves, searching for answers to difficult questions about life, trying new things, or when we are faced with problems. How are you emotionally unique? Can you recall a time when your emotional expression was different from your friends or family?

Reread these lines below from My Emotional and Me.
Emotions are natural and useful for me not weird or strange or wrong or right
Emotions are like a dial I turn that dims or brightens my inner light
The emotional part of me is like my own ready compass for guiding my life
Use the new insight you have received from My Emotions & Me, consider how you can now look at situations differently when your feelings are different from others?

4. Feeling good helps us to enjoy life. There is an easy way to develop a habit of feeling good. Take a moment to think of several things you are good at or simply like doing. Now pick one. When you are doing that one thing how does it make you feel? Now list the feelings you remember experiencing. Make a habit of regularly choosing to do this and other things you enjoy. What will you do first?

5. Making mistakes is a natural part of life and learning. Our **self-talk**, the things we quietly tell ourselves as we make mistakes can be positive or negative. Self-talk also influences how we feel. Do you remember the last time you made a mistake? What did you tell yourself? If it was negative, you can change or improve your self-talk by using the examples below.

A. I made a mistake when I _____, but I forgive myself.
B. Making mistakes is a part of life but because of my mistake, I learned _____.
C. I made a mistake when I _____, but I am not the mistake.
D. I accepted responsibility when I _____, and I can move on knowing things will get better.

6. Being **mindful** means paying attention to how we feel with kindness and gentleness. In other words, don't judge yourself or your feelings as wrong or right. Just notice them. When we notice our thoughts, actions, and feelings we can make helpful choices. How we feel can show up in our **body language**. For example, wide eyes are a sign of shock or surprise. A clutched fist is a sign of anger and sweaty palms are a sign of nervousness. Being mindful can bring us back to a place of calm. Practice one of the strategies below the next time you feel anxious, upset, or uncomfortable.

A. **Focus on your breath**: Pay attention to your breath and observe each inhale and exhale until you feel calmer.
B. **Deep breathing**: Take a deep breath and slowly blow it out repeating as long as needed
C. **Happy Place**: Imagine being in your favorite place for a few minutes.
D. **Break time**: Take a break from the present activity and do something else that's fun.
E. **Truth moment**: Find a friend you can be honest with and ask them to listen without interruption as you share.
F. **Take a walk**: Take a brisk walk in the fresh air in your neighborhood or nearby park.
G. **Listen to music**: Focusing attention elsewhere on music stimulates good feelings.
H. **Drink some water**: Water soothes and hydrates the body and decreases feelings of anxiety.
I. **Count to ten**: While focusing on each number, count to ten slowly this will help to reduce stress, and defensiveness.

7. Our feelings are responses to what we notice with the five senses (sight, hearing, touch, taste, and smell). Additionally, our feelings are a response to the emotions that come from within us. We will have problems, challenges, and joyous times in life but all the while it is our responsibility to learn to be aware of how we feel during those times.

Our emotions are like a close friend who is always honest. Learning to listen to and trust the messages our emotions give us is a way to learn about ourselves. Relax. Close your eyes. In your mind picture the most memorable moment of your day. What messages were your emotions giving you?

8. Love is an amazing feeling. Love makes us feel comfortable and accepted. We often feel love when we are with family, close friends, and special people who are important to us. When we feel worried or are upset, we can remember loving times to make us feel better. Remembering loving times comforts us in loneliness and makes us courageous in the face of fear. Recall a time when you felt loved and accepted. Explain how you knew you were loved and accepted? How can you use that experience to help others feel loved and accepted?

YOUTH AFFIRMATIONS

Making positive affirmations is the practice of positive thinking. Positive affirmations make you feel empowered. When you repeat the affirmations often and believe the words you speak, positive change will happen for you. Affirmations help to change **self-sabotaging** thoughts and behaviors Self-sabotaging behavior is what one personally does that is different from the goals and desire he or she really wants. Read and review the list below.

Choose an affirmation. Perhaps one each day or one to focus on for the week. Speak it out loud or to yourself. Feel the meaning of the words in your heart. See yourself doing it. Repeat this process as often as necessary.

Morning Affirmations

- Today is going to be a great day.
- Today I choose to be confident.
- Today I expect good things to happen for me.
- Today I choose to be happy and feel good.
- Every day is a chance for a new beginning.
- There's nothing wrong with starting over.
- Today I will be aware of how I feel.

Feelings and Emotions Affirmations

- My positive thoughts make me feel good.
- I choose how I feel.
- I am in control of my feelings.
- I am grateful for my emotions.
- I will listen to the messages my emotions send me.
- I allow my emotions to move through me.
- My emotions are useful for me.

Self-Acceptance Affirmations

- I believe in myself and my goals.
- My perspective is important.
- I like myself.
- I am proud of myself.
- My best is enough.
- I only compare myself to myself.
- My individuality is special and important.
- I am an amazing person
- My beautiful is unique.
- I love myself.
- I deserve to be loved.
- I believe in my talents and abilities.
- I can change and learn new ways of being.

Self-Awareness Affirmations

- I am authentic.
- I accept myself just the way I am.
- It's okay if I make a mistake.
- I only compare myself to myself.
- I forgive myself for my mistakes.
- I am aware of myself, others, and my surroundings.
- I am comfortable being myself.

Personal Value Affirmations

- My life matters.
- My life has a purpose.
- My imagination is beautiful and powerful.
- I can make my dreams come true.
- I am meant to be here; I am not an accident.

Courage Affirmations

- Everything always works out for me.
- I can solve the problems that I am faced with.
- Challenges make me stronger.
- I can do whatever I put my mind to.
- I take positive actions in the face of fear.
- I am getting better and better every day.

Care Affirmations

- I care about others and others care about me.
- My family loves and supports me.
- I have the positive words I need to say.
- I am respectfully assertive.
- I care about how I feel.
- I speak kind words about myself.
- I speak kind words about others.

Authenticity Affirmations

- I am beautiful inside and outside.
- My differences are a good thing.
- I am proud to be authentic.
- I am happy to be a unique individual.
- I am beautiful in many ways.
- I love myself and my special way of doing things.

REFELECTION QUESTIONS

For Caregivers

You will need a journal or notebook and pen/pencil to record your thoughts as you answer the reflection questions.

We can learn to understand the emotional part of ourselves. Developing a better understanding of our **emotional self** makes our lives happier and more productive. We can have more rewarding experiences and healthier relationships when we acknowledge the significant role that emotions play in our lives. ***Read the reflection questions at a pace that is best for you.***

1. Take a few minutes to look back at the last week of your life. What was your emotional condition? Each life experience we have is accompanied by emotions. How do you describe your emotional self? Are you emotionally balanced? Reactionary? Apathetic? What if anything can you recognize that your emotional self is telling you about your present well-being?

2. Think of something you do well. Recall the last time you participated in that activity. How did it make you feel? It important to be aware of our feelings when you do well. We often look for approval or praise from others when we do well. How can you use this information to encourage yourself?

3. Now consider the opposite. Can you remember when you made an attempt that didn't work out as you hoped? What thoughts came to mind? How did you handle not meeting the mark? Did you give yourself time and space to emotionally process what happened? What was your **self-talk** like (statements that you thought or made about yourself)? Was it negative or positive? What will you continue doing or do differently next time?

4. Emotions are personal. We do not have to emotionally agree with others. Nonetheless, it's beneficial to **empathetically respect** the feelings of others. We can learn from others when we are aware of our contrasting emotions. At times its best just to **remain neutral, listen,** and **observe.** This is called **holding space** for another. When we hold space, we are physically, mentally, and emotionally present for someone. Holding space is focusing on another without judgement as they express their feelings. All understanding must be realized by the individual not forced upon others. In what ways can you demonstrate that you are respectfully aware of the feelings of others?

5. Our feelings surface so that we can identify our own needs. Feelings reflect our innermost response to what we are experiencing. Consider the most recent conflict you have been involved in. Did you listen to the messages your emotions were sending you so they could help you communicate **authentically**? Did you honor the emotional choices of others or did you demand them to emotionally agree with you? Examine your actions and the emotions that surrounded your decisions.

6. Emotional maturity is attained as we continue in our process of becoming. Because we are always changing, learning, and growing, so is our emotional self. Emotionally mature people understand that **patience** and **self-compassion** create a graceful understanding of ourselves. Further, they know mindfulness is a key component of emotional maturity. Mindfulness requires us to be aware of ourselves from a place of loving-kindness rather than shame or judgment. In this way, we can wisely monitor our emotions and the **emotional contributions** (*how we present ourselves emotionally and what emotions we bring to the moment*) we make. Challenges meet us with family, at work, and in various social situations as we live our lives. Identify three areas where you can become more mindful of your emotional contributions.

7. Everything is **energy** including our emotions. Emotions begin within us and manifest outwardly as feelings. People are often conditioned to think that others control how we feel. However, our feelings are our choice. We may be **triggered or stimulated** in some way by others but our response is our own. In those moments we should practice **self-control** and **healthy emotional expression** rather than **emotional suppression**. Being **authentic**

and honest are important. However, being authentic without healing personal issues like regret and resentment can damage relationships. Honesty without empathy and integrity can be malicious. How can you begin to take personal responsibility for your feelings?

8. Since emotions are energy in motion, it is imperative to maintain a sense of **emotional balance** and well-being by keeping that emotional energy moving. When emotions come up it is important to notice them and recognize why we are having the feeling. Then, allow the emotional energy to pass through us. Blocking and avoiding fully expressing our emotions can negatively impact our well-being.

We are NOT our emotions. We experience our emotions. Judging emotions is a misguided action. Emotions are like street signs that tell us where we are but we use our awareness to guide us where we want to go. What have your emotions told you lately about where you are in your life, or certain circumstance, and where you want to be?

9. Once we notice and identify our emotions, we can allow emotion to pass through us. However, emotions can be both delayed and detoured which usually brings about unwanted outcomes like burdened hearts and sickness. Some ways to allow emotional energy to move through us are as follows: ***becoming present in the moment, deep breathing, physical exercise, venting, talking with a friend, journaling, acts of service, and being creative in various ways.*** How will you allow emotion to pass through you? Choose a different way from one you may have previously chosen.

10. Another technique for productively handling emotions is **transforming or transmuting** unwanted emotions. When we transmute emotion, we find a higher perspective and focus. For example, if someone is feeling down or depressed you can choose to join them in the low place. Misery loves company. Many people join, sometimes out of obligation, in order to provide evidence of care. However, care is still apparent for others and self when we choose to look for the silver lining in the dark cloud. Being a "Pollyanna" (over the top cheerful person), is not the goal but changing the mood so that it is more beneficial and preserves your emotional state is the goal. How can you transmute low emotional energy in a reoccurring situation you are faced with?

11. When we feel good our emotional energy is vibrationally high. On the other hand, when we are feeling down, our emotional energy is vibrating low. However, neither should be judged as wrong or right. Our human experience provides us with inevitable moments of both high and low vibrations. Checking in regularly with ourselves helps to increase awareness of how we feel. What can you do to make yourself more accountable in recognizing your emotional state? Here are a few examples:

Journaling	Take a few minutes to write freely about what you are experiencing. Journaling moves the energy in us and furthers our process.
Meditating	Relax. Focus on your breath. Pay attention to each inhale and exhale. Meditation helps us to be more present and brings clarity to our day.
Daily Self-Checks	Check-in with yourself three times a day or as often as you like. Be honest about the feelings you notice. Then, make a healthy choice for yourself.
Five Sense Focus	Relax. Choose one of your five senses (smell, touch, taste, feel, hearing) and focus for at least 1-3 minutes: For example, focus only on what you hear as closely as possible for 1-3 minutes. Doing this helps us regain our center and refocus.
Gratitude Moment	Think of what you are grateful for. If possible, show gratitude for what has no monetary value for at least one minute. Showing gratitude can shift your attitude.

12. Anger can be an intense emotion and it should be acknowledged as an urgent alert. Because anger is often misjudged as negative, its expression sometimes brings about erroneous shame and guilt. Anger is not our adversary. The emotion of anger is our helper. Anger helps to shield us when boundaries are crossed, protect us if we are in harm's way, and prompts us to object when our personal truth is dishonored.

When we become angry the energy of that emotion has to be resolved in a way that is safe for ourselves and others. We can deal with anger by simply **removing ourselves** from the situation. Further, it is possible to be **assertive** when we are angry both respectfully and authentically. Number 9 mentions ways to allow energy to move through us. Brainstorm some other ideas with someone you trust. Write some examples of how you can allow the emotion of anger to move through you. What will you do the next time you are angry with others?

13. Personal evolution and healing old wounds is possible for everyone who wants to do so. When our pain has not been healed, overtime we have a tendency to continue in old emotional pain because the pain was not fully faced when it happened. So, we carry the pain around with us.

Whenever you are triggered and the pain comes up, place awareness or consciousness on the pain separating it from the present incident. This keeps the pain from controlling our thinking and behavior. Being present with the pain in the now moment with compassion can transform it and bring healing.

Identify a reemerging painful memory that you want to merge with care and compassion. The result will eventually be a wonderful difference in how we interact with others and ourselves.

14. Our feelings play an important role in creating the quality of the life we live in. Our thoughts and feelings broadcast the life we want. What we broadcast outwardly is what we in turn receive. Our inner being always has our best interest at heart and always feels "good". When we ask, it is given to us and our inner being receives the request. However, we have the responsibility of aligning our physical selves (what we do) with our inner being by using our feelings.

In other words, we know we are in alignment when we "feel" excitement, certainty, and well-being not frustration, fear, or doubt. Feeling the former puts us in a space of allowing and vibrational sync with what we desire. The latter puts us in disharmony and pushes us away from what we want to manifest in our lives.

We can feel outwardly the way our inner being feels! Do not take score of the unwanted things that have already shown up in your life. To have the life we enjoy we have to pay attention to how our thoughts and actions make us feel. We create the reality we experience. How can you practice the vibration of your inner being so that you are resistant free in the subjects that matter to you? What good feeling thoughts can you practice about the life you want to live?

Here are some ideas you may want to try: (helps located at the end of the book)

A. Offering pure gratitude in faith
B. Pray an unconditional prayer of appreciation NOT supplication
C. Declare daily affirmations

15. Acceptance and unconditional love are the breeding ground for authenticity. The more that we accept ourselves and love ourselves the more unconditionally accepting and loving we can be of others. Regardless of the state that we find ourselves in, we can learn to lovingly accept ourselves. What part of yourself would you like to be more accepting of? How can you express more **self-love**?

CAREGIVER AFFIRMATIONS

Making positive self-affirmations is the practice of positive thinking. Positive self-affirmations make you feel empowered. When you repeat an affirmation often and believe the words you speak, positive change will happen for you. Affirmations help to change **self-sabotaging** thoughts and behaviors. Read and review the list below.

Choose an affirmation. Perhaps one each day or one to focus on for the week. Speak it out loud or to yourself. Feel the meaning of the words in your heart. See yourself doing it. Repeat this process as often as necessary.

Morning Affirmations

- Today I will fill my day with activities I enjoy.
- Today I will remember my best is enough.
- Today I choose to see the bright side.
- Today I will make the best of every situation.
- Today I will look for humor and fun as often as possible.

- Today I will not take myself so seriously.
- Today I will focus on being a giver.
- Today I choose to smile and be happy.
- Today I will stand in my truth.
- Today I will support and encourage others.

Feeling Affirmations

- I can move through the feeling I am experiencing right now. The feeling will not last forever.
- I can choose a thought that feels better than the one I am presently thinking.

- I am not defined by what I feel. My present feelings do not have to control my whole day.
- I am allowed to feel the way I feel. I do not need permission.
- I am not responsible for changing the minds of others about my feelings. My feelings are personal.

- This feeling is present so that I can become more aware of something.
- I can sit with what I am feeling until I have clarity.
- I choose to bring light to what I am feeling.
- I do not judge myself for the way I feel, especially when it differs from others.
- I accept my emotions and let them serve their purpose.

- Even though I am feeling this way, I am still alright.
- Although I am feeling this way, I can focus on my breath and recenter myself.
- Despite the fact, I am feeling this way, I am still worthy of love and respect.
- While I am feeling this way, I don't need to force myself to feel differently right away.
- While I am feeling this way, I am still a good person. I am not my emotions.

Gifts and Ability Affirmations

- I use my gifts and talents to help others _____.
- I feel good about my ability to _____.
- What I love about myself is my ability to _____.
- I feel satisfied when I_____.
- I am grateful for my ability to _____.

Personal Priority Affirmations

- I give myself permission to be curious and ask questions.
- I put myself first and that's okay.
- I give myself the self-care and attention I deserve.
- I know how to listen to my body and make choices that are right for me.
- I stand boldly in my truth.

Endurance Affirmations

- I will finish what I start.
- I forgive myself for my mistakes and accept that I am human.
- I accept what I cannot change.
- I learn and grow when I face obstacles.
- I know I can accomplish whatever I set my mind to.

Worthiness and Self-Acceptance Affirmations

- I am worthy of love and respect.
- I only compare myself to myself.
- I believe in, trust, and have confidence in myself.
- I know myself, accept myself, and am true to myself.
- I embrace the personal change I am experiencing.

Authenticity Affirmations

- I am beautiful inside and outside.
- My differences are a good thing.
- I am proud to be authentic.
- I am happy to be a unique individual.
- I am beautiful in many ways.
- I love myself and my special way of doing things.

OFFERING PURE GRATITUDE

Prayers often go unanswered when they are offered from a place of need. See prayer **NOT** as a time to offer an earnest plea but to a time to boldly state a declaration of what we know belongs to us as our birthright of abundance and freedom. The appearance and form of this looks different from person to person but the birthright is unconditionally ours.

The prayer is answered or manifested according to the degree that we hold the prayer to be true **NOT** hope for it to be true. Anxiety, worry, doubt, and unbelief have no place when offering pure gratitude.

Our words create the reality we experience. We should speak with awareness. When we speak in the affirmative and align our mind and actions with what we want, the desire will show up in our lives. Offer pure gratitude and watch your reality transform.

PRAYER OF UNCONDITIONAL APPRECIATION

To manifest whatever, it is that you want, offer a prayer of unconditional appreciation.

Use this example and feel free to change it as it suits you.

I love the feeling of clarity, and I recognize how Source/God/Creator/All feels about me. I acknowledge my sense of well-being, security, and contentment that comes through alignment with my inner being. I know I am an extension of Source/ God/Creator/All. I love the feeling of allowing. I like the variety of my experience. Source is with every idea that is birthed within me. I like the feeling of awareness. I like knowing I have access to infinite intelligence. I like knowing I am not alone and I have all the help I need. I like understanding and knowing the value of my being. I enjoy the law of attraction. I like knowing that everything is working out for me.

THE PAIN

Suddenly it happened
Wasn't expected nor imagined or maybe it was
Everything takes place with a reason not just because

Well, whatever the case, it was too much for me to handle
Like clockwork, duplicating my early examples
I would not, I did not, I could not at the time admit
When my actions and theirs did explosively coexist
The great pain and inner turmoil made wounds I could not resist

With haste I packed pain and pushes pain hard deep down under
Unbeknownst to me the pain lay in wait beneath with famished hunger
Creating circumstances that matched its appetite
Keeping me in a habitual freeze or frenzied state of fight or flight

No, I did not grieve
Neither gave myself a chance to believe what was really going on
No time to weep
No time to process nor to respectfully mourn
Nope! Not Now! Perhaps some other day or maybe later on

Hurt is weakness
Too strong and in control for this and that
Quickly finding a reason to rejoice to escape my heavy sadness
Incident made imprint one after another over time for years
Carrying around broken appointments to weep huge buckets of my tears

My pain needed the shining light of awareness and consciousness
To dissolve it to disappear
But no! I had to keep it moving working on improving playing the role and looking the part
Dressing up the outer me
For my pain was not significant nor a personal priority
I had not yet learned
Forgiveness was only part of my responsibility

The dormant pain still lived on festering inside of me
Faithfully distorting and clouding reality
Yearning for a trigger
To remind me of the times I'd rather not remember
Defensively deflecting
Blame game, "It's your fault!
Whining, "Why me? the victim!
Perceptions that my pain consistently thought

Enough with being delusionally comfortably uncomfortable
Now my healing, is absolutely nonnegotiable
No more projecting pain out of me and onto them
Fully present in compassion with the pain refusing to condemn
Finally, realizing there's healing for us all
Our pain energy needs completion and a means to resolve

Dr. Free

RESOURCES

Abraham, Hicks, E., & Hicks, J. (2009). *Ask and it is given: Learning to manifest your desires*. Carlsbad, CA: Hay House.

Akbar, N. (1999). *Know thyself*. Tallahassee, FL: Mind Productions & Associates. Barrett, J., &

Barrett, R. (2009). *The complete Cloudy with a chance of meatballs*. New York: Atheneum Books for Young Readers.

McGraw, J. (2002). *Closing the gap: A strategy for bringing parents and teens together*. New York: Fireside Book/Simon & Schuster.

Cloudy with a chance of meatballs. (n.d.) video, 2009

McGraw, P. (2005). *Family first*. New York: Simon & Schuster.

Puddicombe, A. (2015). *The headspace guide to mindfulness and meditation*. London: Hodder & Stoughton.

Robbins, M. (2009). *"Be yourself, everyone else is already taken: Transform your life with the power of authenticity"*.

Tolle, E. (2004). *The power of now: A guide to spiritual enlightenment*. Berkeley, Calif: Distributed to the trade by Group West.

Tolle, E. (2018). *A new earth: Awakening to your life's purpose*. London: Penguin Books.

Tsabary, S. (2014). *The conscious parent*. London: Yellow Kite.

Vanzant, I. (2015). *Trust: Mastering the 4 essential trusts: Trust in God, trust in yourself, trust in others, trust in life*. Carlsbad, CA: Smiley Books.

Verde, S., & Reynolds, P. (2019). *I am peace: A book of mindfulness*. New York: Abrams Appleseed, an imprint of ABRAMS.

Yamada, K., Besom, M., Bellair, L., & Yamada, K. (2021). *What do you do with a chance?* Fairfax, VA: Library Ideas, LLC.

Yamada, K., Besom, M., Bellair, L., & Yamada, K. (2021). *What do you do with a problem?* Fairfax, VA: Library Ideas, LLC.

ABOUT THE AUTHOR

Deana "Dr. Free" Gordon MS, Ed.D. has devoted her life to guiding others through healing, instructing, and coaching others in the process of transformational freedom that comes through authentic living. She knows that everyone has the inherent potential to live their best life by becoming the best version of themselves.

Dr. Free understands that knowledge of self is the beginning of wisdom. As an experienced educator and leader, she has made a positive impact in the lives of young people and adults for several decades. Dr. Free has worked in public schools in Tennessee and Georgia as well as overseas serving as a classroom teacher, school leader, and parent community liaison.

She has a Bachelor's of Science degree in Elementary Education (Middle Tennessee State University) a Master's degree in Counseling (Trevecca Nazarene University), an Educational Specialist degree (Tennessee Technological University) +30 hours in Counseling and Education coursework, and a Doctorate in Educational Leadership and Professional Practice (Trevecca Nazarene University).

Additionally, as a motivational speaker, she has inspired diverse groups of people nationally from all walks of life to reach their fullest potential. She has served as a spiritual leader in varying capacities for over twenty-five years. She uses her training to remind others that our authenticity is the best gift we can give to ourselves and the world.

Other books by Dr. Free available at Xlibis.com, Amazon.com, and Barnes and Noble.

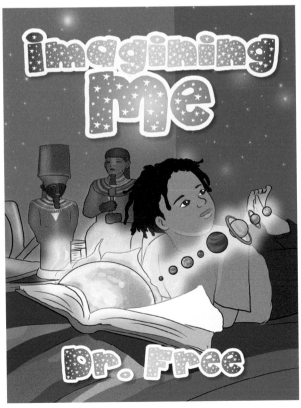

Printed in the United States
by Baker & Taylor Publisher Services